...and it happened
under cover

NightWing Publications
Seattle, WA 98168

© 2013 by NightWing Publications

...and it happened under cover
ISBN: 978-0-9914505-0-3

Library of Congress
Control Number: 2014931468

First Edition

Alicia Winski Rich Follett
Editors

Alicia Winski
Cover, Design and Typography

www.NightWingPublications.com

Printed in the United States of America

for the loving hands and uplifting
spirits who have encouraged and helped
give voice to NightWing Publications

&

for the quiet choir
still waiting to be heard

~keep the faith~

we're coming for you

With much gratitude to the authors who placed their work and their faith with NightWing. To my 'partner in crime,' Editor Rich Follett, I offer my heartfelt thanks for his wisdom and endless enthusiasm, as well as to Marie Lecrivain for her pragmatic vision and advice. I would like to extend my deepest appreciation and thanks to Stephen Roxborough and Dale Winslow, both of NeoPoiesis Press; Stephen for his infinite patience and guidance; and Dale for her generosity of spirit and support. I am so grateful to these people; without them, their kindness and encouragement, NightWing Publications and this collection, so dear to my heart, might never have taken flight.

Alicia Winski

~

My heartfelt thanks to Alicia for opening a new window in my creative world by choosing me to be her co-editor; to Connie Stadler for insisting that I return to Poetry; to Dale Winslow and NeoPoiesis Press for bringing my poems to the world, and to my beloved wife Mary Ruth who, with unconditional love and absolute faith, has patiently weathered the long hours that I have therefore spent huddled single-mindedly over a computer screen.

Rich Follett

FOREWORD

Not too long ago, we were asked what the purpose of this collection was and why we felt the need to publish it. In all honesty, we hadn't delved too deeply into the whys and wherefores of this book until that question came up. The answer, however, came easily: the driving force behind this anthology is a desire to challenge our culture's prevailing attitude that physical intimacies between consenting adults are 'dirty little secrets' to be kept under cover. For a growing number of open-minded seekers, sexuality is a gift that, when openly expressed in caring, comfortable intimacies without the weight of guilt or censorship, arouses not only the body but also the mind, the heart, and the soul.

Alicia says:

As a young woman maturing in a sexually charged and highly confused society, I initially approached my own sexuality in the dark – blind and under cover. Expressing my desires both verbally and physically was an oftentimes shameful and horribly embarrassing proposition. Without knowledge of or confidence in my own desires and sexuality, sex was at best an awkward interaction – rarely pleasing and generally frustrating. However, as I became more confident; more aware – as my world and viewpoints expanded – I came to realize that there is little as beautiful, as natural, or as erotic as the clear and direct exchange of physical intimacy and desire between lovers. In truth, I found the unabashed honesty of these scenarios to be an unexpected (and very pleasurable) aphrodisiac.

Rich says:

As a survivor of childhood sexual abuse, my childhood and young adulthood were spent in the never-ending pursuit of a positive frame of reference for human sexual interaction. The great revelation of my middle years has been a hard-won awareness that the crippling childhood sexual experiences I have long fought to rise above were actually a proving ground for the strong, resilient and passionate man I have become. In opening the door for acceptance and forgiveness of self and others, I have begun to realize (albeit late in life) that there can be beauty and freedom in openly expressed desire – in sexual intimacy. My journey continues. In the meanwhile, co-editing this anthology has been the best thing in the world to loosen me up, to force me outside of my comfort zone and to help me relax into something beyond my former guilty and Puritan shame. "[A]nd it happened under cover" has been a game-changer, for me, in the most real sense.

~

We at NightWing view this collection as a kind of seduction; a titillating paean to open, honest lovemaking where partners can freely explore without shame or fear. We hope that these poem and prose offerings will entice readers to broaden their sexual horizons. We hope that they will inspire readers to explore shared fantasies where even the deepest, darkest desires can be mutually satisfied without guilt or regret. Finally, we hope that they will encourage readers to embrace a new awareness where love can be confidently and joyously exchanged and nourished, brought out from under cover and into the light where love and sexuality *belong*.

Table of Contents

Foreword

Blake said that the body was the soul's prison
unless the five senses are fully developed and open.
He considered the senses the 'windows of the soul.'
When sex involves all the senses intensely,
it can be like a mystical experience.

Jim Morrison

SHE'S IN BED WITH ANOTHER POET

deep under covers
in the middle
of his love

kissing every line
stroking every stanza
moving to
the rhythm
of his breath
through her own

sucking the marrow
of his meaning

each thrust
of holy blood
on the sheets
takes her
deeper and deeper
into his pulse

a private place
where secret perfume
whispers
the church of word
into her

wanting ear

~Stephen Roxborough

HUNGRY

I want to put your poetry
on all fours

lick sweat
from the groove
in its rhythm

roll your
naked syllables
upon my tongue
until I can taste
the salt
of your soul

until I can hear
your deepest meanings
in my flesh, screaming
in my bones, groaning
in my veins, throbbing
I want to feel the body

of your words
upon me
grinding against
my soul

taunting me
with its flow
consuming me
with its lust

until
in cathartic release
I explode into your passion

melt into your peace
hide myself in your warmth
until our shared dream
falls into slumber

as always
knowing I'll wake up
hungry for more

~Niall Rasputin

I WANT

I want to fuck you.
I want to put my cock inside you and move it around.
I want to feel your flesh encircle mine.
I want to put my lips on your lower lips
And taste the sweet salt of your womanhood
Lapping and driving you into a frenzy
I want to hear your moans and see
Sweat slicking your body.

I want to spread your legs
As wide apart as they can go
Your ankles on my shoulders
To enter at first softly, slowly
Then driving with passion.
I want you to be, secretly, privately
The slut that you want to be.
I want you to undress in front of me
Stripping and watching me rise
Becoming rock at the sight of you

I want you to dance
Showing me every inch of your white skin
Opening every part of your body
And I want to kiss every pore
To kiss your thighs, your stomach, your beautiful bottom
If there were ten thousand pores
It would not be enough.

I want to have you kneeling in front of me
Your head between my knees
To feel myself inside your mouth
Stroking your lovely hair
I want you to wear a t-shirt

So that I can pull it up
Pull up your dress
Pull down your underwear
And lean you over a couch
I want to shove you up against a door
Running my hands over your whole body
I want to sit you on my lap
With my cock between your thighs
Cupping in my hands
The doves of your breasts

I want to watch you lower yourself onto me
Watch as my cock vanishes into you
Or spooning from behind
I want to sit by the heater
Legs and cock and cunt tangled
While the light turns your beautiful skin
Into red-gold honey

And then, sated,
I want the best thing of all –
To hold you to me in bed
No covers
My thighs against your thighs
Cock to cunt
Stomach to divine, beautiful stomach
Tender soft breasts against my chest
My arms around you
Hands stroking you
And to spend an hour, two hours, three
Just looking into your glorious eyes.

~Thomas Kent

SPEAKING LOVE

i will blindfold you with words
there are colors in my eyes this night
i have travelled so far to be here
every night dreaming of undressing you
your kiss its breezes down my spine
it isn't fair this separation
how can two souls live apart in love
close your eyes on my departures my love
let me mask you with my tongue
with the light of my breathing
on your closed eyelids
no do not open your eyes

until you feel me whole
until you feel me with you
as i have never been 'til now
til the dark of these months have lost me

do not beware of me
do not hold anything against me
let your arms loose
yes hold my finger
hold my arm
hold my neck
hold my lips inside you
til the poems of your love break free
from open fields of unknowing
be nobody not even yourself
open your legs
open them for me my love
i am as blind as you
only my words are here

to touch you
to lick the lingerie from your lips
to open the night to open the black
to become black inside you
to become bluer than the black of you
to run these thousands of fingers
these millions of blind tongues
over your soft skin
which hasn't felt a man
which hasn't seen a man
yes my love

make the woman in me a man
make the man in you a woman

hold me

don't let me go
don't let me go

~Dom Gabrielli

PROPERTY

1. In the light

I keep thinking about the way
you keep your thumb hooked in
the belt loop of my jeans, like you have me on
a leash, like you own me. I'm not sure I don't like it.

2. In the dark

I lie on top, your skin grazes mine. I breathe
your scent, burrow in your flesh, forehead
flush against your belly, eager
mouth fellating your cock. So this is love!

3. In the even darker
Go ahead. Push me
down. Pin my wrists. Wedge your knees between my
thighs; pry me open. You know
you want to explore my corridor, my
antechamber, my presidential suite. There's a basket
of fruit on my D-cup titties, Veuve Cliquot in my 'fridge.

4. In the winter
You like fucking on top of the sheets, heater off,
windows open to remind us we're still breathing. I
can see your breath, its smoke - and mirrors.

5. In the cut
I keep thinking about the way
you keep me under your thumb.
"Yes," you say. "This *is* love."
And I'm not sure I don't like it.

~Alexis Rhone Fancher

WAR GAMES

no rules apply here, in this arena where
games are held & militant players meet,
inhibition abandoned to merciless collision

frenzied hand to mouth combat, textured tongues
tangle, all teeth & claws, blood drawn,
wounds sweat-stung

parched mouths seek oasis, sipping splendor
where life expires, reborn in paradise met
with fierce engagement, a coveted encounter

mad dogs howl, vying for position,
[alphas in conflict], clash, bone to bone, proud
flesh under siege capitulates to savage hammer

a willful prisoner taken, held captive, *[holding captive]*
a captor, warily shackled together, a draw conceded,
champions undefeated in these nocturnal –

war games

~Alicia Winski

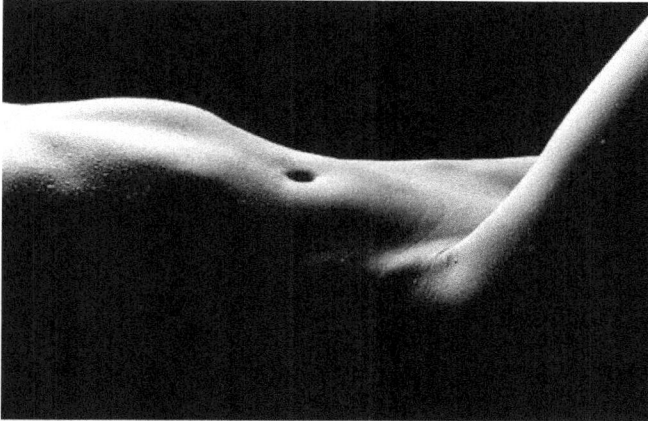

SILK AND VELVET

I kiss the spot where
Silk hides intimate velvets
Between her sweet thighs

~Phil Maguire

SWEET

Forehead roll,
the fashion of a teardrop
joyful finds itself pulled,
down to the nexus of septum,
slow curve proboscis to lips'
open fall, chin and swan dive

To the chest, nestled
in the tight cleave valley
of the dew kissed hills,
taut into the lowlands

Just before the darkened forest,
ascent from honey on the wing,
drop caught fast on pink protuberance
he tastes salty sweet and works his way up.

~Rose Aiello Morales

WHAT'S LEFT OF WHAT'S RIGHT

i take the strong mint
from your mouth & plant it
somewhere
south

      somewhere in the center
of your pleasure
& blow until the heart
of your heaven
heats up

      steal an ice cube from
your drink & ease it
from instep over ankle
past your calf

            up your
        inner thigh
    into a quiver shiver
& devastating
sigh

up up up
ever so slowly
to your delicious lips
suck
      what's left of what's right
& drink all of you
into me

~Stephen Roxborough

BEYOND TOUCH

my body in your body
the tongue of sun running
light waves to the horizon
of we two rising and falling

the opening of the world
the eruption of universal thought
sound spills ripe over
every awakened contour

your body in my body
the fingers of moon urging
shadows to lick the secrecy
of we two plunging boundless

~ Dale Winslow

LOVE AT THE MEDITERRANEAN

The sun was lemon-shaped
over the Mediterranean,
and I,
young and salt-less,
walked its back,
walked its neck
with her.

Gul told me,
somewhere along the wet ear,
Only people
in love
should see the sea,
but I already knew the water
in a defiant way, knew that love
had changed along the beaches,
just as her hair caught
the spray
and she laughed
into the spring morning.

We went to eat fat strips
of bread
with goat butter,
shining,
as we watched all the early souls
toast and fry
in the light.

If you say so, my warm lemonade.

~April Michelle Bratten

OXFORD GERANIUM

You shift the world
With your words
Salacious pearl

Voluptuous Geoid
A raw frenulum
Of black leather
Clasping pink mammilla.

Oh, Oxford Geranium
Forget not your hat—
Xochiquetzal's
Black bowl
Dripping milk
From her skin and bone.
To the lips of
The Amazon--your mouth.

~Alan Patrick Traynor

SEX NIMIS MULTI PRO SONNET

I am a smiling cat when I lie next to you
I feel your hair warm against my face
Your whole body still as the quiet earth
From sky-dreaming head to rooted toes
I sniff your cheek and think of exposed
Skin while you sleep so I instinctively kiss
Your sweet smell on the warmed blanket
Let you inhale more breaths as I caress
Sense your pulse on my wrist, your heartbeat
On my chest, or is that mine communicating
With you on an animal level in our bed
As a car honks outside the window, light
Fills the blind cracks while my hands roam
Your pajamas for a breast, my fingers play
With a cloth-covered nipple, I nuzzle a lobe
You cough and sigh, my nose ingests you
I hug my muse, close my eyes, having
Taken notes for a poem on a folded piece
Of paper which I toss away and proceed
To recreate again the experienced poetry

~Don Kingfisher Campbell

LIKE A VALENTINE

Bubbles from chilled champagne
and effervescent laughter
rising up from his depths
into the nape of her neck
as he licks salty sweat
and bites down
without breaking skin.

The marathon of touches
gentle, deliberate,
teasing, tingling.

Hips moving
in sacred rhythm
to synchronized beat.

Final collapse.

Deflated sighs
before the spooning
and into the
arms of Morpheus.

She wakes alone
in tangled sheets
like every other morning
in this empty house.

No body next to hers.

No champagne bucket
anywhere in sight.

No crystal glasses
on the bedside table.

No morning note
on the pillow.

It must have
been a dream,
another taunt
like others before.

He is never
coming home.

He would if he could,
but he probably can't.

Animal sounds
escape her lips
as she claws
at the top sheet
with unbridled despair,
shaking it
as if to death.

She stops mid-snarl,
blinking her eyes
at the pink,
faded from red,
men's briefs
she sees in her left hand —
like a valentine.

They belong to him.

His magic briefs
he swears he will
keep forever.

She sits perfectly still
clutching the pink.
Somewhere
between her racing heart
and silence,
between prayer and doubt,
fact and fiction,
war and peace
the smell of bacon frying
drifts up from the kitchen.

He is home.

~Barbara Moore

AWAY

The motel room door is locked. DO NOT DISTURB sign hanging from the door knob. Inside, the room is dark. Little candles fight impotently against the darkness on tables and dresser tops, aggressing and regressing against the darkness like little old tired fingers. The floor is strewn with clothing. A skirt. A belt. A pair of work boots. A pair of underwear. A shirt. A high-heeled shoe. A pair of pants. A sock. Panty hose. Panties. Bra. Other clothes lie in other places in the darkness. There are whiskey bottles and little plastic cups. There is a bucket of water there, with ice cubes floating and giving themselves over slowly to the devouring tongues of water and heat and time. There are empty packs of cigarettes. Cigarette butts bloated and disintegrating in the bottom of empty beer bottles. There is a wallet. A digital clock, red number flashing 8:00. Two cell phones. Some assorted change scattered about. A set of car keys. A set of earrings. And two wedding bands.

In the bed, two bodies fumble and grope for each other and find each other like blind people. They are all hands and mouths. All fingers and palms. In the darkness, it is hard to tell where one begins and the other ends. Where man stops and woman starts. They are two shadows melting into each other and forming symmetries of imperfection, unions of flesh forged in a bed of tangled sheets, out of the reach of God and his perfect design. Out of the reach of bad dreams and warm milk and homework and neighbors and lullabies and bedtime stories and time clocks and phone bills and upset tummies and husbands and wives and phone calls and bad days and giggling and headaches and backaches and menstruation and sleepwalking and anything that can happen to stop this from happening. Here they are all alone. Here is a universe all their own. here they are two gods. Here the bedsprings can creak and crack and lurch until they explode. here they can roam the floor in full nudity. Adam and Eve. Here they can scream and laugh and moan and cry and scream again until their lungs ache from the act. Here, whiskey breath can have its way and each forbidden word can have its say and there is nothing they can't do, in this room.

There are a hundred different things he wants to do to her. There are a hundred different things she wants done. And they do them all, and the clock ticks away minutes toward 10:00 when all things

21

will once again be as they were. The clock ticks, and they work harder at each other, until they wring each second from each minute and leave it lying on the floor with their clothes and shoes and other things. He turns on the lights. She blows out the candles. He puts on his clothes. She puts on her panties and bra. Pulls on her skirt and blouse. he puts his wallet back in his pocket. She puts on her earrings, her shoes. Fixes her hair in front of the mirror. He picks up the change, his car keys. He takes his wedding ring, slips it on his finger. She slips on hers. They give the room one last look. They smile at the mess of it. They step out the door. She opens her cell phone. Gives the babysitter a call to let her know they are on their way. They get into the car.

Together.

~Verless Doran

VIATICUM

Then,
as now, my beloved,
(some sixty years on)
I let my thoughts drift to you
in a white cotton nightgown…
billowing guilelessly in effortless gossamer grace;
illuminating even the most mundane morning rituals –
parting the curtains,
          peeling potatoes,
                    preparing chowder –
you were,
          you *are*
          the only poetry my life has known or needed.

When the war raged;
when the bombs fell;
as my banded brothers
found Heaven's gate;
          day after hellish day –

every wisp of cloud-white gun smoke,
every white-hot spray of shrapnel
was a fold in your white cotton gown –
a sail come to waft me away
to the sweetness of our chowder days
and remembered home.
Lately,
I am in need of your billowing sails more and more;
I meander aimlessly through rivers of memory –
through fields of echoed agony undimmed by time –
scanning the howling horizon for any sign of peace,
hungering for release.

Soon, I think, it will be time
for billowed sails and safe harbor;
until then,
      light your lamp, my white-winged angel —
stir once more your sacred stovetop salvation:
I will fight for one more day;
I will shout back the darkness;
I will crawl on my belly through the killing fields;
all for the touch of your hand…
all for the poetry of your white cotton gown…
all for the chance to savor your chowder —
rich;
creamy;
sweet;
life itself —
      and you
the giver.

~Rich Follett

DO YOU REMEMBER HOW SHE BROKE
YOUR HEART?

Was it a soft gesture
a simple down turned smile
that stray lock of hair that would never stay in place?
A faded green pair of panties that never seemed to leave the floor
or find their way into the wash?

Was it the first three notes of her favorite song.
The way she held her fork in public
Or just watching her move when she didn't know you were there?

Do you remember
feeding each other grapes in a nameless park,
somewhere in the shade
knowing this time you might not make it
knowing this time it all might hit the ground
knowing
you loved her?

Remember
watching her put her clothes on was more mysterious
than taking them off
touching the small of her back while she walked beside you
the muscles in their own rhythm, her feet, so small next to yours?

The warmth she left behind whenever she got up to go to work
like lying in a forgotten sunbeam
stretching and catching her looking at you

The look
in her
eyes.
Buried where they can't hurt you

in quiet spaces
behind quiet faces
you try to forget the first time she touched your mouth
the first taste of her sweat
the red backed journal where she kept her private thoughts
the one you never opened

It's all there if you'd only show it
the cracks on the road less traveled
the slow pace of her breathing as she slept,
draped across your body on the couch like your favorite blanket,
tv flickering,
touching her ribs
the smell of her hair
rich as life.
Buried where they can't hurt you
in quiet spaces
behind quiet faces
you try to forget
fingerprints on polaroid
flipped over onto her back
puckered exit wounds like ripe flowers on her body
her arms at her sides
the blood strung down in red ribbons, dry and vacant
all the bruises and scratches

I try and I try
...but those eyes
staring up
filled with nothing
It always comes back to pain
That silly little fucking hat they put on her
to cover the hole in her head at the funeral parlor
That silly little fucking hat she'd never wear in a million years...

cringing in the shower
rocking and rocking
moaning and crying
shaking and sobbing
but there wasn't enough water in the world to wash away the tears
the pain squeezing and squeezing and squeezing...
Blinded in a white hot sheet of pain
you try to forget anyway,
and remember just a moment
holding it tight

when she danced
when she laughed
when we loved.

~Hart D. Fisher

TRUE LUCKY LOVERS

DURING THE WINTER oranges are cheap
and plentiful and bananas too
i love to type the word bananas, it's a wonderful little dance
if i live it it makes it life, even while it lived
appears and disappears.

if you don't like the weather wait 5 minutes it will change
as fast or slow as it wants to go, it's all just leftovers.
these electrons can be fun

i just wanted to get into her panties with her and my oranges
i was shy
but my bananas are ripe enough to make a pie
and so that's what she did, she made a banana pie
we spent the next forty years in bed at least once a week,
and sometimes i cheat and say it's twice a week

~E.L.Freifeld

I WANT TO MAKE LOVE TO YOU, SHE SAID

i want to make love to you, she said
beyond the surface grime
of superficial touch

i want to penetrate you she said
deeper than a bull humpback's
full moon moan

she said i want to rock you until
we roll into each other's DNA

until we exchange cells & selves

i want you tangled & sealed inside
she said so you'll carry me
everywhere

you'll lift me to your lips
with every heartbeat

& every time you raise a glass
or even if you make love
to another

i'll be there she said

to float & glide each step
of your dance

embrace your every thrust
& breath

~Stephen Roxborough

READING FRANK

soiled by melancholy
she encloses her body
within healing waters

a wine glass perched on the shelf
her head reclines on an inflated pillow

and in her hand
a spark of his unnatural fire
smolders and then burns

igniting the embers
in his eyes

highlighting the reasonable
furrow of his brow

and the prurient spectre
of his pedestrian shame

the water warms as his desire
is slowly and rhythmically revealed
steam rises
and sweat beads between her breasts
she pulls the plug and the waters recede

the metaphor of him
strides into the room

she remains as dirty as before

~Marie Lecrivain

DELICATE SUGGESTION

Dry lip heat
the tongue rolls languorous
white teeth sparkle dew,
a tip withdraws into its secrets.

Lash flutters on a lower lid,
a feather kiss upon its own skin,
butterfly sheds powder softly blue
upon a small river of black line.

Rearrangement on a velvet stool,
one leg crosses at an ankle
a glimpse of paradise, an eye
drawn by an artist to a faint light palette.

A nail taps slightly on a fresh flush cheek,
across a room a trap is set, then down around
a glass' rim, an upturn of the Fates, surround
as sound grows dim except for footsteps walking.

~Rose Aiello Morales

NOW YOU SEE HER/NOW YOU DON'T

oh I see

they must have arrived
and for now
I am gone

erased

acknowledged,
but best
not mentioned
noli mi tangere

I am accustomed to anonymity
to slipping in and out of sight
to invisibility

but if you want to
hold me

you may want to
keep me

where you are
able to

see me

~Nancy Davenport

THE BLOUSE YOU TOUCHED

I didn't wash the blouse you touched for two weeks
later I asked you to touch my words in a magazine
I held your arm and you said 'that's a nice touch'
we touched we touched
and the waters of our lives pulled us apart.

~Lois Michal Unger

VIVA VOCE

foreknowledge
is never enough
inside my mouth
are languages
you cannot hear

I put you gently
between my lips
pull you in slowly
deep into the wet
and warmth

so that you might
understand
these words
I cannot say

so that you might
discover
what you will never
be able to tell

~Dale Winslow

FLASHBACKS

I have flashbacks
of him and me in those count 'em on one hand times when we were
precisely in sync, and
we fucked like a well-oiled machine
drilling, filling,
spilling. oh
I have flashbacks
of him and me in those I'll never forget 'em moments when we'd
climax together
a single being
for a second. A blink.
When I felt safe.
I have flashbacks
of him and me surrendering... No. Me surrendering
him observing, packing it away for later when he needed
something on me; something
like my vulnerability. My perversions. My secret heart.
I have flashbacks
of him and me, see us naked, on the bed,
curved into one another, his body pressed into mine,
his penis already hard against my ass,
his long, black leanness, protective, like he has my back.

~Alexis Rhone Fancher

CHANGING INTO SOMETHING COMFORTABLE

After years of folding underwear,
noticing it has become noticeably bigger,
where has all the drama and excitement gone?
Where is the *out damned spot*?

After all changing and turning old into rags,
where is the mystery? Where is the intrigue?
Where is the saucy lady and six-pack man?

All gone. All gone away and shall not return.

Where is the see-through and barely there;
is it because there is too much there?

After seeing the underwear spin in machines,
and displayed on mannequins, where
is the acceptance into growing older
and the only time it is off is on a clothesline?

Where is the passion? Where is the passion fruit?

Tonight I fold the cups into a promise. I fold
the boxers into a belief something will happen.
Tonight the slip will slip off into a dramatic pose.
Tonight the sock drawer will applaud.

Isn't it grand to still be lustful? To still desire,
with lights on, all the flaws of growing old together?

I drop the underwear and become unaware
and fold into her arms, getting what is necessary.

Tonight we will wake the neighborhood up.

~Martin Willetts, Jr.

SHE KEEPS A GUN IN HER PANTY DRAWER

it's a dangerous place to go
rummaging around
so I keep out of it most of the time
she doesn't keep a diary
or some such nonsense like I do
and I hide mine out in the open
but she does keep a gun in there
just in case
of a prowler, or a rapist, or something more dangerous
like if I'd been drinking and get too grabby
or violent –
she has the power to silence me
right there in her panty drawer

I'm assured that it is fully loaded and chambered
a slick bi-tone SR9c from Ruger
that fits perfectly in her hand
and I can assure you that she knows how to use it

she doesn't wear it like she does
the drawer's other contents
which run the gamut from everyday wear
to Friday and Saturday night under the silken dress wear
they all turn me on – including the gun
knowing that she knows how to use each one of them
to deadly effect.

~Jhon Baker

BLUE

my wristwatch on my desk is a perfect parking place
for my pipe
leans nicely at 70°s for swinging in a hammock
and making love underneath the trees

for every good lay there's a time and a place
you dreamed you would be

meanwhile i've been invited to a panty party
can't help thinking whose panties to attend!

but ah, how can i ever forget the one that got away
if i could only remember the color of her panties, that day.

funny, i think they were violet
no
red,

red is better and rhymes with her bed
and violet i would never forget

who cares if it's true
i wished she wasn't having her period that day

who cares what color they were
who cares if it was true
then i realized i blew it!
when she said 'but dahling,
you didn't even notice,
my panties are blue'

~E.L. Freifeld

PANTIES

Panties here and panties there,
some call them their underwear.

High cut thighs, bikini style,
these are sure to make you smile.

Some are thongs and some are lace,
these will cause your heart to race.

Some are crotchless, some see-through,
we all know what these will do.

Some are satin, some are briefs,
but all are passion's handkerchiefs.

~Timothy Reed

BETTIE PAGE, QUEEN OF THE PIN-UPS

Bettie Page, Queen of the pin-ups,
knew the secret to a man's heart
was not letting him see everything,
but a little here, a little there,
and then beware — it was off
to the races.

Bettie knew hints
were better than full disclosure.
A daring peek, a seductive glance,
still keeping him guessing.

She knew
men unfolded her picture at night
and what happened after.

It was alright —
a little imagination went a long way.

Bettie kept them busy guessing.
What was it she was hiding?

Bettie made her lips cherry red,
puckered a hidden promise
she would not keep, and kept it.

Naughty, naughty, her eyes said.

She crossed the mystery of her legs.
Men sighed across continents.
The camera eye ogled; steamed.

Variations of underwear posed.
Seduction is knowing how much
of a good thing is too much.

~ Martin Willetts, Jr.

PROVOCATEUR

provocateur
you know what you're doing
roping me in
with your verbal skill
your talented tongue
toying with me
winding me up
leaving your mark
all nails and teeth

playful and confounding
gasoline on the fire
laughing it off
trafficking in words
seductively so

turnabout's fair play
just keep it coming
and

nobody

gets

hurt

~William Kowalski

YOU'RE RUNNING AFTER ME

You're running after me he said
No you see the thing is I have too much pride
He looked at her with a winky sort of look
She looked at him with black dress
and breasts
And a whole body beneath the dress
And wondered what she should read into a winky look

~Lois Michal Unger

EQUINOX

when she calls I run
meet her within the hour
we are dope smoking mothers
last night of freedom
as his texts
plot his way home
we talk love lives
mine
hers
mine
hers
she snapped up the perfect man
at a bargain price
he didn't know his value

on the open market
we talk sex
she is an oceanic flood gate
release the sea
me drought struck dunes
sand drift in the wind
i tell her
i've always loved her
i try to rub against her
at the red light but again she says no

~Coral Carter

A CHANCE TO GET AWAY

Mike was happy when Heather said she and her paralegal were going to a conference in Chicago. He and Heather had been married for eleven years and mike saw it as a chance to get away by himself for a while. Their relationship no longer had that excitement of the first few years, but they had grown into a warm, comfortable place together. Heather and her paralegal, Angela, would be at the conference for a week so Mike arranged a week off from work. It would be a break from the daily drama and petty power plays of the insurance company he worked for.

He decided he would go visit his best friend, Allen, in New Jersey. Allen's house had been damaged by hurricane Sandy and it was Mike's first chance to be with him after the disaster. Allen was fortunate; his house had only minor damages, but other homes on the block were completely destroyed. This made winter in the seashore community even lonelier. Mike thought it would be a good time to see his friend and boost his spirits.

When the time for the conference came, Mike dropped Heather off at the Philadelphia International airport. She was flying out with Angela, a flirty, twenty-four year old blonde paralegal. He hauled Heather's over-stuffed suitcase to the valet and kissed his wife goodbye. "Call me at night after dinner and have a great visit with Allen. Tell him I say, 'hello,'" she said. Mike then drove to his friend's house.

Allen and Mike spent a quiet week together. They talked, read, drank beer, ate pizza, watched basketball on TV and just "hung out."Mike called Heather every evening after dinner. Mid-week, Heather, always careful not to judge another person, hinted that Angela was acting like "girls gone wild." When Mike called Heather on Friday, she didn't sound right and said she wasn't feeling well. She had a headache and nausea and was staying in the hotel room for the last day of the conference. Mike knew not to press her when she wasn't well; it only made her cranky.

When Mike picked her up at the airport he knew something was wrong but Heather just said she was still feeling sick. They drove home in silence. When they got home, Heather went straight to bed. Mike, feeling sorry for her, began to unpack her suitcase. He was about to close it when he noticed something in the side pocket. It was a pair of thong panties wrapped around a bulbous black dildo and a note: "Thanks for the wonderful week. Love, Angela." A thick red lipstick kiss was at the bottom.

~ Phil Maguire

EYESHADOW (for Alicia)

girls splash eye shadow in the spring
after long winter underwear and sweaters
blue skirts red skirts white yellow
smile at the reflection in the mirror
girls splash eye shadow in the spring

~Lois Michal Unger

EDEN—PARADISE UNDONE

No one knows love like the young man in his sister's bedroom.
He knows love's heat like cats know the sun.
Her drawer is open he sighs, chooses …
He touches her smooth satin bra
with the reverence of an acolyte,
slips the hooks into the eyes behind his back—
a practiced art (he's done so a hundred times)—
then, kissing his fingers,
he tucks himself in and
chooses violet panties to match the bra.
He is thin, a fragile creature,
and the violet satin moves up over his flanks
easily.
He counts to ten in a whisper
then turns to the mirror.
He poses, smiles,
breathes in the scent of *Aqua Allegoria*
The very idea of this preening is illegitimate.
He knows.
His heart is full of love and he imagines Eden.
His senses are ripe
His hands
reach toward the mirror.
"Come," he says to his reflection,
"come with me."

~Martina Reisz Newberry

MOTHER'S LINGERIE

Midday in all direction,
I feel wrong, wrong, wrong
about my mother's lingerie
flying in the air,
her drawer burst open
and whatever she keeps searching for,
perhaps a letter,
a jilted mirror,
not there, not here.

I poke and touch,
touch and poke her underwear
and feel the blood runs
midst those cups and triangles,
and her blood whimpers and whines
chased by some unanchored pain.

I duck my head and meander
through those apparels
all stuck in midair,
all wrong, wrong, wrong.

~Kushal Poddar

IT'S ALL IN THE COLOR

"It's all in the color", she said, her beckoning, beguiling
scarlet tipped fingers slowly, shamelessly stroking a tiny,
silken string in an alluring appeal to the senses, a provocative
invitation; a private party waiting to be crashed; crushed by
wanton, wicked whispers

it's all in the color

a thin strip of white purity deceptively innocent,
disguising multitudes of sin under the stained,
pallid sham of dancing Madonnas, while pink is pretty in lace;
coy, kittenish youth peeking out from under stark, dark
affectations of prim maturity

yellow cotton sizzles as hung sheets drying under
the neon gaze of hot, scintillating summer days scented
in blooming narcissus springing to life the withered roots
of ancient trees to proud attention under the warmth
of a friendly caress, but red—

"I think red is your color"

blood red, commanding, demanding attention;
take me, make me, break me;
a bright slash of scarlet branding a pale,
smooth canvas in bold pronouncement-
not for the faint of heart!
there's no purring kitten here-
-no sir; there's a tigress in this tank and she's ready to roar

a smokin' hot nasty siren ripping through a quiet night;
a dazzling comet shooting 'cross a blue velvet sky;
a bullet train racing down a slick track;

a hot rod shooting out from the starting line
at zero to ninety in no time flat,
engine screaming, tires squealing—

> *I got it, you want it,*
> > *come and get it*
> *that's it, yes, yes!*
> > *red! red is my color!*

tensed in conversion, a sweet slip of violet discarded
in quiet descent down quivering thighs, forgotten,
pooling around parted ankles trembling in anticipation,
an expectant silence breaks under the weight of an answer
to which there can be only one question

> *"shall I ring you up now, or*
> > *can I interest you in a matching corset?"*

~Alicia Winski

LITTLE BLUE DRESS

gauzy cornflower
hiding eager gems
drapes soft silken stems
midst spring's hazy glow

gnarled canopy blinks
dappled rays on their press
clenched miles past caress
fistfuls of milk curve

black lace hooked aside
hungered unbuckle
fingered honeysuckle
drips rippled rhythms

part ways atop leaves
search the sky ever blue
eyelets folded in dew
push-pull in pulsed heat

double-knotted surge
caught in crimped pleats
dust drumming beats
pounding chorus of

yes
yes

electric increase
sunset a timepiece
sweet nectar release
'neath that little blue dress

~Michele Shaw

NECESSARY ALTERATIONS IN COLOUR SCHEMES

Chantilly douses herself in dusky pink,
Sherri in powder blue,
the girls had style and style had the girls, regularly.

All that gaily colored plumage in the bird cage,
teased & preened, perched crossed-legged
on mahogany furniture & rumpled satin.

Mary always leaned toward olive green,
Alice to chartreuse, Kate to amaranthine . . .
colors write themselves into psyches & beds
Sophia to jade, Bridgette to gentian,
Juanita to verdant . . .

The seamstress sews using one slender digit
adjusts hems and seams
drags the thread from the head
to the estuary with delicate proficiency.

The last gasps are always ones of wonder
as the spider veins dance along the fallen ledges
smeared in aubergine.

~Teri Louise Kelly

I WANT LOUBOUTIN HEELS

I want Louboutin
heels with those trademark red soles,
I want them sexy, I want them high.
I want them slingback and peep-toed
so I can flash the purple polish
on my tootsies. I want to wear them
out of the store, just you try and stop me.

I want to wow them on
Washington, saunter past C&O Trattoria
and Nick's Liquor Mart, those bottles of Stoli
stacked in the window, calling my name, past the
summer-clad tourists in December, shivering,
barefoot, like LA has no winter.

In those shoes I'm hot,
stop-a-truck hot, prettiest
girl in school hot, and this
time, I know it.
Flaunt it. Hell, I own it. In those shoes I can
pick and choose, not settle for some loser.
Not drink away regrets, pound back Stoli at
Chez Jay's, flash their scarlet bottoms when I kneel.

I'll wear them like my own flesh,
like hooves, like sin.
I'll keep their secrets, won't spill
where they've been.

Better those shoes with their lurid soles
than you with yours.

~Alexis Rhone Fancher

SHE GOT GAME

she got her game on, a warm night,
air bristling with static-cling anticipation,
a smooth operator accessorized in a sexy
slip of a dress black as a night ocean
glistening over the depths below—
a mystery waiting to be uncovered

a hidden treasure--
        aching to be discovered

she got her game on, lips blushed in rose,
mysterious eyes shadowed in tea leaf green,
a hot lick of red waves and baby smooth skin
deliciously misted with the subtle scent
of Temptation lying-in-wait behind lacy
innocence sheer as a fine dusting of snow topping

the mounds of
        soft, sloping hills

she got her game on, a night at the movies, playing
blind man's bluff in the dark, sly fingers roam pale waxed
columns languid under the siege of a bold adventurer tracing
the moist outline of luscious lips burgeoning against
a near translucent resistance

all barriers breached,
    demands set and reached

she got her game on, a quiet moan escaping
the mouth of Eve, dew kissed digits are
withdrawn from lush pink petals

with a soft, satisfied sigh, she settles back against her
buttery popcorn seat triumphant with the discovery
of wealth hidden behind a sexy slip of a dress
and beneath it—

    a wisp of white

she got her game on …

~Alicia Winski

SHARE YOUR SECRET WITH ME

you're delicious in papaya pink
spaghetti straps on honey shoulders
warm in golden light
such a luscious peach
a feast for the senses
no man could resist
your sinuous beauty
careless and abundant
deserves reverence
and adoration with no limit

~William Kowalski

UNTITLED

Sometimes
You wake up when you shouldn't
In your bed
In darkness.
Hungry darkness
Choking darkness
Eager darkness
Lying there
Eyes open
Moving
Liquid darkness
Leering darkness
Burning darkness
Easing
Deep into the belly
You stare
Not seeing
Standing by your door
Watching your chest rise and fall
Tasting the nickel on skin sweat
Cold
So fucking cold
I stand there
Rise
And fall
Rise
And fall
Fingers tight
You lick your lips
Slowly
I touch myself

In the doorway
In the dark
I hold a piece of you
In the dark
We rise and fall
In the dark
Horns are hidden
In the dark
Standing in your doorway
Moving like a tongue
Softly
So softly
Your chest
Rise
And fall

Rise
And fall
In the dark
Sometimes is a lonely place.

~Hart D. Fisher

DISRUPTION

Do not be deliberate in this love.
A deliberate love
will kill us both.
A jury deliberates;
passing judgment
on the damned.

Be accidental;
accidental as lightening,
as an orchid.
Sanctify me with your utter
lack of order and
routine.

Do not give me a calm love.
When the sea is calm,
it can be deadly.
The forest floor claims its dead
calmly.
Have pity on me,
I want to live instead.

Slap me awake.
Shatter me.
Scare me.
Quit waiting for my permission.

Kiss me.

~Lisa Alvarado

WOULD SMELL AS SWEET

no matter
where

he scents himself,
my lover

smells sweetest
at the

crook of his
elbow.

~Nancy Davenport

FROM ACROSS THE ROOM

from across the room I know what underwear she is wearing
I study her closely whenever she walks or stands still thinking
and I often imagine her without such clothing
down to her silk and lace – red or black
translucent and revealing

I think she knows this and often will wear
the sexiest bra under standard t-shirts
just to turn me on as we go through the normal day
so I am left wonting in every moment
for the sweat of her thigh
or the caress of her breasts

and it is always why I walk behind her
following like a puppy dog who hasn't eaten
in a week
but lived off of coffee, several cigarettes
and imagination

at day's end I watch her drop her worn attire
to exchange for playful pajamas
which I'll try to remove as the evening passes

~Jhon Baker

DURING MY LUNCH HOUR ON YOUR DAY OFF

The sun's glistening granules rained
down on us, made small indents
on our bodies made into one
by kisses so profound, my
eyes ached.

Blanket, a public
park, your hands excited and
not knowing what to grasp first—
settling on my hair—all this
I remember, will always.
Such history won't be veiled,
though God knows I've tried.

That park
is a parking lot now, I
know that. But our ground lies
underneath, the bright sand of
our sun still lights it.

Our kisses
still bless what is there: the force
of scandal, of silence, and
the eternal weather
of almighty passion.

~Martina Reisz Newberry

THE GIGGLE SCREAMER

You can tell a lot about a woman by what sounds and expressions she makes during intercourse. And if you are incredibly perceptive, you may be able to tell what sound and expressions a woman makes while getting her brains fucked out by knowing what kind of person she is. I once had a friend who thought he could tell what a woman is like in bed simply by looking at her. Honestly, I rarely thought he was very accurate at all, but I never told him that. Instead, I encouraged him each time by overtly entertaining a supposition that he was spot-on. This game of his was far too amusing for me to ruin it with something as trivial as honesty.

Hell, before I met Barney, my daily lunch break was 30 minutes of lock-watching agony; sitting in the shopping mall food court devouring my lunch while pretending not to notice the far-away glances of teenage girls in demeaning uniforms, and while trying not to stare at all the wealthy housewives fishing for attention in thousand-dollar outfits, their meaty asses swinging like pendulums or the pocket watches of hypnotists, their silicone-enhanced milk-melons bouncing like beach balls in the ocean, each of their contours attempting to pop a seam in a garment so as to reveal its full beauty as pale flesh glistened in the artificial light. I would sit alone with my gaze affixed to my lunch as though it was the entire universe as the seconds trudged along like geriatrics swimming in Jell-O. And then I met Barney.

Barney worked at the video game store. While I folded clothing and monitored the dressing rooms for thieves, Barney played first-person shooters on a demo console and discussed video games with geeks. By the time he went on his lunch break each day, he was suffering from hardcore porno withdrawals, longing for the video collection at his shitty apartment like a crack-head longs for one more hit. this dirty little game we played offered his filthy mind an outlet for all that sexual energy so that he could make it through the day without his balls exploding.

I recall one day that Barney was locked and loaded by the time he sat across from me with his tray of food.

"See that cougar in red? She's a bossy teeth-clencher—all like, 'More to the left! Faster! Stick your finger in my ass!'—until she orgasms. Then she clenches her teeth because she thinks screaming is a sign of weakness."

I laughed so hard that Diet Coke sprayed out of my nostrils.

"And the blonde at the pizza place with the pizza face? She smiles like she's staring into heaven because she's thrilled that someone's actually fucking her. And that fine-ass Japanese girl approaching screams, 'Hai!' because 'hai' means 'yes.'"

"No, she's a giggle-screamer."

"You question my ability?"

"Hi, Lloyd!"

"Yukiko! How do the new panties fit?"

"The same as when you put them back on, silly."

~Lloyd Dobbins

BLUE SILK PANTIES *(to David)*

Blue silk panties
... were a token you once gave me,
a contract between us to be *yours*
at the height of the witching hour.

Your hands on my hips;
a sign of dominant devotion,
the heat of your desire burned
against the soft barrier of indigo
that you slid down my legs
& tossed away to be lost
amid a tangle of sheets & limbs
while your blue eyes searched mine
for signs of surrender
as I caught my breath
in time with each upward thrust,
the erotic interlocking
of our bodies alchemically
conjoined as we lost ourselves
in the blue heart
of the Flame...

I awoke alone
in an empty bed
with leaden limbs
& a blue heart,
now wrapped
in those same silk panties
that rest in the bottom
of a dresser draw
gathering dust.
~Marie Lecrivain

INVISIBLE SYMPATHIES

The old boy didn't know nothin' about panty sizes or bra cups and all such as that. Hell, with a man's underwear it's how big around your waist is. It ain't nothing can't be figured out with a tape measure. Women got all these different numbers and letters and dashes and dots and he didn't know whatall. But she had told him she wanted something she could feel sexy in, so he come walking into the Victoria's Secret, all 6 and half feet and 270 pounds of him, mud on his boots, dirt under his fingernails, greasy cap with folded bill pushed up high on his head in the manner of country people.

A young pretty girl came over to him. Smiled big. Asked if she could help him.

"Yes ma'am." He said. "I'm looking for some little something-or-other for my wife to wear at bedtime." "Of course." The girl said. "Any idea of what she likes?" "No ma'am. She just mostly wears a t-shirt and jogging pants to bed."

The girl laughed a little. "Well." She said. "We don't sell t-shirts and jogging pants here. We've got a lot of other stuff though." The old boy ran his fingers up in under his hat and scratched his head. "I don't see what's wrong with what she wears to bed." He said.

"How much were you looking to spend?" "I don't know. I don't know how much such as this costs." The girl smiled. "Come on back here with me", she said, "and I'll show you some things."

She led him to the back of the store, passing all kinds of negligees and bras and panties and a lot of things that he didn't even know what they were called. There was all these lacey things dangling from racks and mannequins and posters half naked and some of them more than half naked, some of them a right smart close to being all the way there. The old boy walked through all of that, trying not to look like he was looking. He shoved his big dumb hands way down deep into his pockets, for fear that one might accidentally rub up against all that.

"Do you know what size she is?" The girl asked."I surely don't." "Is she about my size?" The girl stepped back so that he might get a look at her. "They Lord, no." The old boy said. "She's a right smart bigger than you are." He pulled his hands out of his pocket, held one up in the air to about his chest. "She's about this tall." He said, and then his big dumb hands made her shape there in the space between them, top to bottom, side to side, all the ways around. The young girl smiled again. "I think I have just what you need."

She went further into the back and brought him something and he didn't even know what it was called, but it had a lot of lace and things on it, and looked real fancy, and he thought it would work. He paid the girl and she wrapped it in purple tissue paper and put it in a little lacy red bag and handed it to him, and big clumsy fingers reached for it and took it and big dumb hands that had never felt of lace before carried it out to his truck.

#

He didn't think she was ever gonna quit crying. Locked herself in the bedroom. Wouldn't let him come in. Wouldn't say nothing to him. She just cried. Hell, he thought he'd done a good job. Bought her that thing to wear. Give it to her. She tore into that bag like chicken going after a June bug. Got it out and held it up and smiled real big. Turning it over in her lap, holding it up to her cheek. Couldn't wait to go try it on, she said. Went into the bathroom.

And that's when it got kinda crazy. She lit into crying and wouldn't stop. He stood there at the door, trying to get her to come out, but he didn't know what to say. "What's wrong?", he just kept asking. But she wouldn't say.

He went and got him a screwdriver and pried the door loose to where he could open it. He opened it and she was sitting there on the bed. She had the lights off, but he could see her.

That lacey thing was all ripped and tore and stretched on her. She'd tried to get it on, but it was too small. Tried to get her big self into it, but even an old boy like him knew you can't pour ten gallons of water into a five gallon bucket. She looked at him, crying. "It's ruined", she said.

He came a little closer. "Naw." He said. "It looks alright to me." She kept on crying.

He came closer. "Don't cry." He said. "Hell, I think that's the way it's supposed to look."

"It ain't." She cried. "I'm too fat." He stepped closer. "You ain't too fat." He said. "You look just the way I like ye to look."

She kept on crying and he kept on coming closer, and his big dumb hands didn't need the lights on to find her there in the darkness.

~Verless Doran

UNVEILED

there's a place on her face
he could gaze at all day

the line where her upper lip
meets skin just above it

how it dances when she talks
moves him as it waves

captures his awareness
conjures private thoughts

carries him to places
he cannot go by himself

~Stephen Roxborough

SINCE YOU ASK

Any vein that starts at the base
of my throat will lead you there.

Trace one with your finger, down
to where the skin grows pale and full.

Behind the ivory ribbon rose,
my pulse point emanates the scent

of sandalwood or musk. Tell me
which essence you wish to breathe.

I'll make it come true. My nipples
are neither brown nor pink but

a watercolor blend of both
and so soft when your fingers

pass over them, it will be as if
through warm air. You wonder

about the weight of my breasts.
Imagine a pair of thrushes,

their light wild bodies
coming to rest in your hands.

~Leigh Lambert

I DRINK AT THE ALTAR OF YOU

I drink at the altar of you
Your back arcs in ecstasy
As thunder clouds hide behind
Ancient Mountains

Your eyes glorious Gazanias
As the nib
Of me navigates you
Searching – searching

I scallop your bottom
Thirsting in this
River of my desire

An arid lusting
As Jets leave your nail marks
In the sky

And this is for me a
Selfish sustenance
 My cravings - this lascivious hunger
For you my love

For you.

~Roger Cornish

THE VIEW TO LAND

driftwood swept,
foam and sand,
pulled her from the surf,
she clung to me
and I held,
breasts cold wet
panties damply clung,
pushed away she ran,
sand clung to feet,
bent over hands on knees
watched as she lay down
hair lengthened out,
limbs taut,
breasts flattening,
flesh prickled cool,
I wished to run
be upon her,
yet all I could do is watch
with the exhaustion of one
who does not have to chase
anymore,
as lifting hips
slipped fabric from that
place
I would be one day

~Chris Lawrence

LA PETITE MORT

... why, why, why did you need him?
where was I? Just how close to you is he?
(from Kandi by One Eskimo)

you, you were far, far away and he--
he was close, oh, so close and he--
he looks in my eyes and he--
he calls me baby and he--
he makes me want to drop where I stand
and he takes me and he breaks me

all night long

he burns me from the inside out and he --
he rips the flesh from my bones with his teeth and he--
he gets me sticky and sweet, licking me clean as he calls me

baby, baby, baby
all night long

he sings his whiskey warm song in my ear,
it's good, oh so good and he--
he smolders when he looks at me and he--
he pours his dirty little secrets into my mouth
drowning me in a flood to my senses as he--
he overwhelms me with his

baby, baby, baby
all night long and he—

he says all I've been afraid to hear and he—
he turns me to liquid, sipping from this deep,
deep well until it implodes, touching me in places

you can't reach and I die a little death with him

all night long
all night long

~Alicia Winski

IN THE RUINS

sleep then with your hand on my leg
with your finger pointed toward the words
which gather to serenade your fantasy

how many beers sunken on the rock of lonely prayer
these palms open
it was there you danced
yes it is there i long to be
in strange frenzy

i will
i will speak of the future
i will make it now
i will make you

you will give me the wheel
you will hold every muscle of fatigue
it will shudder the evening
so often ever lonesome evening
it is that blackness you wanted
to cancel out the lies of the day
to pummel the hypocrisies

what you feel for will be given
in the vacuum of non thought
it will rise to greet
you have blind hands of feeling my love
you have a hundred fingers
you are the goddess of lips of tender lips

by now the car is stopped
by the old gates to the abandoned farmhouse

we have turned off the light
we have turned off ourselves
we came here for that
for a piece of each other shared and tasted
it is impossible to sit
it is impossible to stand
the uncomfortable positions make the joyful openings
all the more welcoming
for all my spells and hilarious confetti of scattered conjecture
all the words we utter
all the songs we sing
partake of the film no one will ever see or hear
it is ours to share
you are mine to love
what i have for you is mine only in flesh
because it is you who bring me to life

thus i am dead and live
i am conscious with you of being other
and the stick of non being
which you so eagerly lap between tongue and lip
strives to perform its own dance
its own mute tango in transe

here by the roadside
here under the falcon's nested aegis
you will relax all the muscles in my body
you will take me to heaven
in fact you will bring heaven here my angel

soon we will be naked
i will have discovered the depths of your happy desire
we will last long past our deaths

there will be no one
because what we do is invisible
and when animals play
there is no disgust only joy only the you only the I
we throw away
and find
in the same unique instant

~Dom Gabrielli

I LOVE YOU SILENTLY

I love you silently
when you return late at night
in darkened rooms
cats crying outside
hear your footsteps
and babies

~Lois Michal Unger

OLIVES, BREAD & WINE STAINED PANTIES

We ate olives, bread
    With the bottles we mass-murdered
Olives and bread, your lips
    The taste, the wine.

You toasted asagio bread
    I pulled the cork
We learned each other's
    Topology with noisy Braille
Kisses between nips and sips
    Of another dead magnum.

Ever the muse,
    When I spilled shiraz
On your thighs
    Staining your lace,
You laughed
    And I cleaned you like a cat.

You later killed yourself
    With a lost and dog-eared
Notion, or maybe it was I
    Who died

So you could run back
    To your Mediterranean
Moon, and pale mornings.

They matter not, just the
    Taste and texture
Of olives and bread
    Keeps me glancing

Towards the door that
     Stays open, and the
Wistful corkscrew.

~Daniel Armstrong

THREE NIGHTGOWNS - haiku triptych

i.
homespun cotton shift
sixty years: her sail, his ship
one horizon calls

ii.
crimson baby-doll
florid infidelity
tart candy apple

iii.
blushing negligee
ingénue's hope chest treasure
honeymoon draws near

~Rich Follett

ELEMENTS OF LOVE

Your fine hair
As it brushed past my face
Had the sound and feel of
Sand as it trickles through fingers
And blows in fine spun gold over the dunes

The rustle of your dress
As it slipped down from your hips
Reminded me of
The wind as it stirs the cat-coat rye grass
In the high plains, with the distant
Blue-shadowed mountains tipped with white

The sound of your hose and your
Silken panties
Crimson as your heart but
Deep dark and glowing
In the dull light from the hallway
As you stepped out of them
Were the distant murmur
Of a deep midnight sea

The shadows flickered on your body
As you slid into the bed next to me
And the sound of sliding cotton
Ignited fire.

~Thomas Kent

FIRST DAY OF SPRING

Perched on my legs, weightless,
you leaned back as far as possible,
stretching your spine to heaven,
disclosing a welcome gap,
smooth skin, a country to explore,
then you pulled my hands up
to your belt and said, "Undo me …

~Leonard Orr

THE GEOGRAPHY OF INFINITY

as the sun goes down i dream
of moving into your landscape

how my peninsulas fit
into your harbors

how our bays ebb & flow
our tides pool & mingle

how our continents shift together
make peaks & slowly drift apart

how everything vibrates & aches
flows shakes grows quakes

radiates & moves matter
into space that never ends

~Stephen Roxborough

SPINDRIFT

in the stillness
             after
        our wild tide crests,

in the wake of our
             breathtaking one-ness,

i hold her close
             but cannot
        hold her long ...

     between surges,
                  i am

          parched;
barren;
   in her billows
        once more,
                  i divine

destiny -
        eternity -

     bathed in grace
                  on the cradling bosom
             of each coupled swell.
churning in rhythm,

     charting a course
                  in this crescive
        ebb
             and
                  flow,

we cleave
　　　　new shorelines -
naked, virginal
　　　　　crescent sextants

with which we see
　　　　　　all life and
　　　ages to come.

~Rich Follett

ONCE THIS HAPPENED

once this happened:
admiring the movement of her nightgown
above her bare breasts
 - nipples protruding
sensing her sex
I became erect
and took no chance to disguise
but pushed her down and
made easy love

~Jhon Baker

ELEMENTS

It's a cold earth you roam, lost in yourself,
lost to humanity, lost to love—
your steps immune to the scalding ground quivering
beneath scornful feet, immune to fires you vanquish
with a frigid glance

Have you not witnessed the fury of an erupting volcano?
Have you never been singed by the heat of lava flowing
through dry fissures in its race to meet the sea?

Fire ~ Water

Opposing elements clashing, creating between them
a stealthy mist, an insidious vapor slipping in and out
of one's thoughts, melding in that volatile place where

all water flows in the same direction

Singular slow trickles deceptively mild, conjoined,
turned high velocity currents sweeping lone,
abandoned hulls into roiling seas, flooding the void
between them, saturating, expanding dry tinder
rocked wildly beneath the weight of healing waters
leaving a finite voyage softly concluded

Exhausted vagabond vessels wash up onto gritty terrain,
becalmed, left to simmer under a sunburst glare

all water flows in the same direction,
while steam ... rises ...

~ Alicia Winski

JERICHO

Tied to the four posts of his bed,
white silk shed in faux surrender.
I tremble with expectation,
the chilly winds of caution
thrown no farther
than a heartbeat.

I am the sharp blade
ensconced
in the rapists hand,
using the user;
seasoned by stale promise.
Sentinel guards the door
that beats entry.
I crave sensation;
I'm addicted to wet.
My Judas,
the exquisite pain
of penetration.

This is war.

He cases my body,
searches for an angle
of attack.
A silent prayer
burns beneath closed lids.
Callousness finds flesh
made freshly dew dampened.
He tenderly maps
the battlefield
of slopes and curves.

Whispering at the walls
of Jericho

.~Diana Butler

VIRGINITY

You can embrace me any way you like.
Raw, quiet, from below or from behind.
You can embrace me any way you like,
You'll leave no grand impression in my mind.
While you're enclosed within my tight, wet sheath
You can take me there, or, in that other place
The one that's tighter still, concealed beneath
The rounded flesh of my desire – my face
Doesn't change – not really. My mouth – watch! - curves
To shape that *O*. You want to lay the claim
To the tidal wave cresting along my nerves -
Crash together. We do, but all the same,
When it's over. I'm still a virgin in my soul,
We need unfeigned devotion to make us whole.

~Marie Lecrivain

I'LL NEVER FORGET

The dissension prompted an unraveling,
    galvanizing a flood of perilous emotions
    to dissemble the forces that protect the nucleus:
        stigma, embarrassment, humiliation, fury.
    Memories submerged in folds of skin awakened,
        while nightmares wreaked havoc,
          burying my pearly essence
            in a lacquered pine box.

My ego fractured into scattered shards
    like remnants of sand dollars
    abandoned on a lonesome beach,
        where the tide strips sand
        from the barren shore.
    Dormant reflections morphed
        into a torrid hornet's nest,
        festering inside my butchered brain,
          as feelings fragmented into aberrations,
          causing the balance of power to shift
        within my beleaguered landscape.

Tears avalanched, scalding my rosy cheeks,
    as I tasted pungent salt in my mouth.
    Fleeting flashbacks flooded with increasing intensity,
        as my sorrow evolved into a colossal crying jag,
        the shattering betrayal escalating,
          shifting the blame,
          resulting in bewildered guilt.

Recollections of his callous touch emerged in my mind,
    how he caressed, then dominated my unblemished torso,
    how he forced me to perform stupefying acts,

admonishing me for my wicked weakness,
bullying me into vociferously declaring,
how much I desired him, savored him, coveted him,
how I seduced him into devouring my pristine soul,
as I lay facing a grotesque, smudged wall
that displayed a poster of Mary, Mother of God,
embracing her baby, Jesus Christ.

Malicious thoughts surged and seethed into consciousness;
the squalid sheets scarred, while the rancid odor aggravated,
causing me to wretch on to the soiled blanket,
compelling his depravity to ravish my frail carcass
yet again, and again, tainting my faith.
I have become a slaughtered pig roasting
on a revolving spit in the blistering heat.

I shut my eyes, the oppressive sun searing
through dusty slats, as I shut down,
the palpitations subsiding momentarily -
slightly, like a truculent heartbeat trembling —
so that I can breathe and decipher
the genesis of this wicked visitation,
but I am unable to determine the source
that bludgeoned my senses
into sleek submission,
like a concert pianist reluctantly performing
Debussy's Arabesque at the bidding
of a merciless madman.

How can this barbaric uprising emanate
from repressed sentiments that once protected?
How can I walk stealthily amongst the masses
without the risk of shame annihilating my composure?

And will I ever imbibe some gracious potion
      that grants serenity from the bruising events
      that have permanently defaced my past,
         altered my present, and taunted my future?

No, I'll never forget. I'll never forget. Ever.
    My sanctuary has been desecrated,
    the grotesque sins of the boogeyman
       forever looming in conciliatory dreams,
      gnawing at flavorless flesh.

           I'll never forget.

~Michael Wayne Holland

ALL WE ARE

eyes infusing
kiss holes lock
molting cloth lies
tongues roam silk
breath upon nipples
walls aflame
at the pith
of passion's
power
serpents tangle
planets collide

lips all whispers
hips all screams
thunder roars
a feral howl
from lust wounds
bleeding love

problems scatter
as sunlit shadows
anger melts
like ice in spring
long dead colors
bloom again
illuminating
all we are

~ Niall Rasputin

KISS THE COBRA

Transfiguring light
standing naked in the mirrors
of your writhing DNA
light coruscating kundalini
up and down the spine of existence
your language is wind
torrent of your voice
blowing through me

making love among the lilies
blooming in graveyards, making
love in the mirrored iris of your eyes,
making love among the tombstones
of philosophy, our dancing footprints
laced into the shores of time,
making love in the death calamus
beneath the bridges, frantic fucking
upon the alleyways of moonlight,
kissing my feet, sucking my toes
for you
   they were succulent nipples,
nibbling my ankles, chewing
my arches, my soles, my instep
nibbling behind my knees,
lapping the sweet nectar
between my thighs

you were the Unholy Ghost
i was the Virgin Mummy,
Blessed Virgin of the Dead,
    dead to my craving
    dead to my passions
        then I kissed the cobra
           fiery loins shrieking, *"ignite!* ...
Blakean archangels exploding the dam

100 million birds nibbling the yearnings
writhing deep within my sultry nest
        "... ignite sweet pain of passion
            scorching inside me, sullen
            owl-eyed Archangel of Light!"
Crystalline wings
entwined as angels
    shimmering light
    in ice fields of fallen empires
    reverberation breath filling history
as the Greenland ice sheet melts, our
diamonds' reflections dance naked,
two shivering verses elegiac
   commingled as conjugal poem
      there among the shards of men
      there upon the wheel of Time
         singing fractured syllables
         of love and longing

the probing tongue of human DNA
scriptures the world's great suffering
while a single human kiss conjoined
brings to earth all the torments of life;
your teeth devouring my flower's petals
your lips sucking starlight from my cunt
gnawing at my nipples, gnawing my heart
straight-razor to my wrists
liberating the hot red light

you hooked me with your talons,
mounting me, you rode me hard;
our furious thrusting, thrusting,
thrusting amid the stars, in the
moonlight, until I gasped and begged
the grave to cover my nakedness
until my nipples sang, my psyche swam
and my lips tongued the cobra
swallowing the tomb's embrace

you took me in the Tao
slit the winding serpentine worlds
you spread my pounding wings
engorged with blood and moonlight,
the lashing head of your snake
my hissing, striking, seduction;
its lips meet my lips, my flicking tongue
blooming, its teasing fangs poison me

forever with unrequited love
and now i long for you always
in dark transcendental light

~Michael Annis

NICE TO MEET YOU

Fertile panties hit the ground.
The groin runs red, feverish
with hallucination...
drill me.
drill me.

Bodies stare together, un-jointed.
Howling.

~Jessica Wilson

POIEPLEGIA

what i want
is to be luminous, sweeping;
to leave behind verses
translated from candlelit
palabros de amor.

what i fear
is that death,
when it finds me,
will likely find me
still pulling shards of art from
the feet of my puritan shame
(i have never
been able to write
from the waist down).

what i dream
is that
when i wake up tomorrow
the inside of my head
will be *sexy.*

what i seek
is macchu picchu;
what i find
is glastonbury.

what i hope
is that next time 'round
my pen will drip metric love juice
onto linen;
in this incarnation
i am lemon juice

on parchment,
wanting heat and light
to bring out
my deeper
meaning.

~Rich Follett

EXPECTATION

Her contour softened now,
black lace teddy with snap away crotch,
never worn,
hidden under white cotton undies.
There was a time when she hoped.

Ten years of his grunting bulk,
she still got expectations.
Lovers emerge from a hand held shower head.
Some soft, some rough.
They lick, kiss and fuck to her liking
until she shudders.

She slips into bed smiling.
He turns away
thinking of pole dancers
in red lace teddies
with snap away crotches.

~ Cristina Umfenbach-Smyth

PANTY

A misty lingerie hangs from a string
between shutters of the window.
Nothing seems more tranquil.
My house.
My floor.
My room.
If you ever leave this place
I shall keep the panty hoisted
waiting for the world to unwind.
The triangle
to the unfathomed dimension
swings a little to the sound of wind

~Kushal Poddar

NINE LIVES

Sleek as a cat, these black silky darlings
I begin to pass up, considering instead
the old standard cottons.
Then I remember those days I could make your fur
stand up just telling you the contents of my lingerie drawer.
The feel of them, I'd whisper. *They're black and lacy.*
Then I'd say no more, watch your eyes dart down,
then away, that dreamy look you'd get, returning.
I describe my newest purchase.
Years melt away in your lowered eyes
and I whisper prayers of thanks to the gods of silk
while apologizing silently to Hanes.

~D.d. Spungin

BLAIRE

On the university campus in 1968, having Her nipples show through her shirt was considered sexy and Blair accepted the cascade of admiring glances as her inalienable right. her nipples were almost always erect, her body in near constant state of arousal – helped along by the middle seam of her jeans mercilessly rubbing against her sensitive clam on the half shell.

Yet when she engaged in carnal quenching with her dispassionate boyfriend, there was nothing tender about it. Sex filled a need, plugged a hole, and it often took place in the dark. She might as well have been wearing pantaloons for all he knew or cared. But she wore no underwear at all and stuck with the basic jeans and shirt. Easy off; easy on again. Hard as she tried to fool herself, she knew something important was missing.

It was during macaroni and cheese day in the cafeteria, right after she broke things off with her unimaginable boyfriend that Blaire was inexplicably drawn to a feature on bikini panties in an open and abandoned issue of Cosmopolitan Magazine. She had to have a pair. As the day progressed, so did her desire for the lingerie, until she could think of little else. After sitting through Diplomatic History without hearing a word, she decided to skip the rest of her classes and visit Pandora's Box, a tiny shop she'd heard about, tucked into a block of stores not far from campus.

Along with exotic feathers, lace blindfolds, French ticklers and other pleasure-enhancing merchandise was a soul-stealing selection of lingerie. The satin smoothness of the first camisole she held to her cheek besotted her. After half an hour of playing touchy-feely with the garments, she left the shop with a lavender camisole and a pair of deep purple bikini panties. A bit light-headed with anticipation, she made her way back to the dorm.

In her room, she slid Laura Nyro onto the turntable and lit some Nag Champa incense. Removing the items from the pink and black bag, she hastily disrobed and stepped into her new lingerie. While standing before the full-length mirror, she felt transformed. And lying back on her familiar bed, she luxuriated in an unfamiliar afternoon of delight – a satin and silk caressing of self, lasting hours that felt like forever, as wild orgasmic rushes seized and released her body.

Much later, flashing a lopsided grin, as she posed once more in front of the mirror, she made a promise to herself. No more settling for "easy off; easy on again." The next man in her life would be one who could appreciate a slow striptease with the lights turned on, enjoying the fancifulness of flimsy lingerie – someone who could heighten her fantasies with a few more of his own.

~Barbara Moore

UNDERLYING

Thank you for your message.
Have you ever heard of the butterfly quiver?

I'm glad to hear you had a good weekend.
Even if you have, let me tell you about it.

Mine was good too. We didn't get the rain you did.
A woman can strengthen her vaginal muscles

The mountains must've caught the clouds,
by squeezing and releasing them several times a day.

kept them from coming east. I raked a dozen
I do it religiously. If you are ever inside me

bags of leaves. As I write this, more are falling,
and on the verge of coming, you can stop moving,

catching the day's last light as they drift to
hold still, let me squeeze and release you

the ground. I wish we lived closer to one another
as I simulate the flutter of butterfly wings.

so we could meet for coffee and to share poetry.
You'll feel as if your semen is being drawn like nectar

Oh, well. Write when you can.
from your body. Would you like that?

~Leigh Lambert

PANTY HAIKU

harmonious tone
blushing night notes
rhapsody ablaze

~ marlene elisabeth lennon

riding the shaman

kiss
  of scales set close
  to forked flicker
  slide of curve convex
  concave
  this undulating want
  slip of serpent dance cross
  supine white
  rough familiar touch
  of snake to sand
  sidewinder kiss
  rigid lick of heated tongue
  darting
  dance of shaman
  thrust
  fire circles
  leap
  deep swing of curved sweet
  glide of tongue
  to whispered breath
  quick plunge of tasting
  pull of aching wet
  grip and sway
  hard length of hot
  pulse
  strain of urgent
  stroking
  tight rise of fire
  spine undone
  tracing tips cross swelling
  shudder

sharp exhales meet
meld
inhales joined
tight slide of serpent
dance
fervent fingers in
dampened dew
lips to heat
bloom of weeping nectar to skin
salted curve edged
by glide of tongue
lingering taste
of white heated
swells

~Dale Winslow

FRAGMENTS SPOKEN SOFTLY
IN A BLUE PAINTED ROOM

"This morning
newspaper said ecstasy was clawing
its way back into the city."

It haunted your ear like a ghost.

       "Christ is in a bottle
       over on the dresser,
       can you reach him?"

And then --

You closed the blinds,
lock the windows and doors,
and you shook the crumpled paper
from my arms.

~Stephanie Bryant Anderson

A VIABLE SALVATION

sinew aflutter
dusk dope pervades
night verve calls
chaos to worship
tongue flick
carnal nip
biotic bonfires
come howling
sanguine ebb rising
visceral pulse
dream threads
and limbs entangled
a fractional pop
of the frictional charge
revives opiate hallelujahs
at sub-basement depths
of the massacre mind
into bygones
dissolve stacked corpses
as we lie in the aftermath
humming with praise
in a cigarette smoke benediction

~Niall Rasputin

WHAT UNDERWEAR DOES WHEN NO ONE IS LOOKING

Underwear keeps dark secrets.
You can learn much from a discarded pair.
When hope springs eternal, underwear collapses.
There is a spring in the step.
Underwear reveals suggestions of light.
A peek-a-boo is a hint of coming attractions.
The tabloids investigate dirty laundry.
There is much to be learned about the habits of nuns.
Underwear speaks in hushed tones, in ruffles,
never tongue-tied, always tugged.
Sometimes the lace panties run off with the briefs.
They cloister in rendezvous in seedy motels.
Sometimes, for secret passion, they read Gideon's.
Sometimes, they tell each other their kinky secrets.

~Martin Willetts, Jr.

SCIENCE

My *fovea centralis* spotted her beautiful countenance
The *cilla* in my *alveolus* danced at the sight of her butterscotchy
epithelium
Epinephrine started to travel all over my biological unit
Every *Haversian canal* within me vibrated as my *solar plexus*
I couldn't stop gazing upon the summer smooth *clavicle* of her
statuesque *gladiolus*
The *pons* of my brain began to go insane at the vision of her
Fibonaccian *conchas*
She had perfect *maxilla zygomatics* like a model above her *mandibles*
Even her bangled *carpus* was gorgeous; I ran digits over her *ulna*
And happily found our *nares* flaring jointly with joviality
Hoping she wouldn't notice the *occlusion* of my *rictus*
I commenced to lick the *philtrum* above her luscious *orbicularis oris*
I could see *intercostal muscles* move in her chest as I cradled her
lovely
bony *occiput*
Proceeded to stroke both the sexy *ilium* and *ischium* of her
delightfully curved *coxa*
Fondling her supple long *rectus femoris* led to caressment of her
exquisite *patella*
When I reached the gentle slope of *soleus,* I knew I had to turn to
the lovable *mons veneris*
After exciting those *glans* beyond the *perineum*
It was fun feeling her *gluteus* flex and my *trapezius* quiver
As the *synapses* in our *cranial cavities* mutually signaled *dendrites* to
acknowledge *intracellular* ecstasy
My *smegma*-covered *vas deferens* injected *spermatozoon*
Followed by very welcome *diastolic* reactions of the *cardio*

~Don Kingfisher Campbell

TOUCHED

Our second meeting, an outdoor lunch,
we brought sandwiches and manuscripts
and sat formal and stiff at a park bench,
dressed for an office. At our first meeting,
over coffee and poems, our hands (awkward
hands!) had touched accidentally five times.
When we left the restaurant, you touched
my right shoulder to point out a daytime moon.
At the second meeting, we made an unexpected
tactile leap. You looked up from reading
to find me watching you; I wondered why
you held your neck exactly where
it disappeared beneath your thin sweater.
It was the poems, you thought; the *candor*
made you *so warm*. You fanned your face.
I reached across to hold your wrist; I don't know
how I was so heroic. I felt your pulse. I tried
to recall the name of that triangle at the
base of your neck and could only remember
from Ondaatje's *English Patient,* as I touched
there with two fingers of the hand not
feeling your pulse and said, it is called
the *vascular sizood*. Wind blew our two
piles of poems together and you squeezed my
fingers. The next day, we had our third meeting,
new poems to share, and you told me,
as you touched the triangle on my neck,
Doctors call it the suprasternal notch.
But vascular sizood will do for us.

~Leonard Orr

SERENDIPITY IN SIZE '7'

Lugging heavy books from the library
I lumber under the dim
light of the lamppost
towards my dorm room in Boyd Hall of West Liberty college;
the *bibliotheque* is now closed and my brain's toggle switch
is now in the 'off' position

...Upon opening my dorm-room door, I am gruffly greeted
by harsh light and a harsh sight
of silly frat boys
giddily asking my party—*yes* / study—*no* roomie Trish
for a pair of her delicates—PANTY RAID!!!
an *Animal House* moment, to be sure

With a grain o' grace, I muster a grin
(a grinchy grin)
and wordlessly whirl in slo-mo to exit *tout de suite*
Halfway across a cool drawl of darkness,
(i.e., the quad at night)
I remember a forgotten textbook that I need;
Foundations of Linguistics must be lonely on the bookshelf,
I muse in my mind...
geek-stepping double-time back to Boyd Hall to retrieve
the turgid tome,
I am struck
by a man child mob
crowded under the college union lamppost
--or rather , I am struck by the sight
of clueless frat boys oohing and ahhing over
a pristine, petalpink, satin G-string
(belonging to *me*—not my devil-may-care roommate)

being held up high , trophy-like...
What the FRIC (ative) ? I think
Miffed and mortified, I hurry by
feeling very much like Molly Ringwald's
classic character in *16 Candles*

...Candle wax drips of decades later,
my college-sweetheart husband and I
chuckle over the 'under-guchies-in-the-spotlight' incident;
wry smiles
a-flicker

~Gloria J. Wimberley

DREAMING OF FLIGHT

Slow moving fog invades our city -
minds taken hostage
have forgotten the feel of the sun.

I sit within the comfort of a chair which cups me
as a cocoon havens possibilities.

I watch as she slides one bare leg,
then the other, out the open window
till she sits perched upon window's ledge,
sixteen stories above a city that never rests.

My white linen shirt hangs loose over
her delicate limbs – it blends
within the contours of the fog
that moves into her as she inhales.

I can almost hear fog whisper – "leap."
Her hair drips over her – as if
it were an extension of my desire –
over subtle curves that wait to be awakened.

For the moment, she has forgotten me –
she communes with a call few willingly hear.
She dreams of flight – of unfolding her wings –
of abandoning gravity.

I arise – cross the gulf that separates us –
I encircle her waist with arms that could bend steel
or lift a swallow gently into its nest.
I warm the back of her neck with a kiss that lingers
with the hunger of a dream remembered upon awakening.

Her body surrenders a small tremor that stirs my own surrender.
I lift her from her perch, careful not to crush wings.
Head nestled into my chest, her dark eyes coil around my being
as my dexterous fingers slide my shirt from her shoulders
the way sea-foam is reclaimed upon collapse.

I bend – kiss the v of her neck – stealing breath.
I taste the salt upon her collarbone.
My lips moisten the mound of her breast – still cupped
within a robin-egg-blue bra. Her heartbeat
becomes words in my throat.

She leans inward – that silent language of want.
I kiss her lips – her bra falls from sight,
the way wine disappeared at the last supper.

My eyes drink her – no words intrude upon the moment.
Only breath, held and released over lapsed time.
Both hands slide beneath her panties
cupping her waist and hips.

I begin to lift her into the air – to fly once more
as her last garments drift to the earth
with the gentleness of a feather giving up flight.
Raising her over my head – she spreads her wings.

I lower her – just a fraction – a kiss held long.
Then we are two golden eagles twined
within the other, with no fear
of the oncoming ground.

~Duane Kirby Jensen

LEONARD COHEN BLUES

Inauguration Day: I'm sitting on the couch, flinging thongs at the TV screen. My grim tells me the Fin del Mundo virus is still hanging on. I'm waiting for the bank emissary to email me back the status of the Cash for Keys Scam. Her Polish sounding last name turns up an art degree. And, I imagine, a gap in her front tooth I'll only see after the first vodka.

She's living in San Diego, working and walking among a ruthless beauty she loves and hates. I'm one of 25 she's cashing out. I'm guessing I'm the friendliest because she writes back promptly.

\#

It's been a couple hours. I'm over us meeting and discussing the mountains of the 19th century and her penchant for girdles. I'm into my third episode of Cold Case Files. Semen and panties like carrots and peas. I can't stop watching.

\#

Next day there's a number in my landline directory: New Orleans coroner. What do they want? I don't call them back and I'll tell you why: semen in panties - short shorts, really. I left them in a hotel room on Orleans Street in January of 2006. I didn't mean to leave them.

They belonged to a woman I met in a deserted hotel bar, a looker from Shreveport, tiny waist, bulbous behind, loved drinking hurricanes. Few of those later, we're dancing big figure 8s.

\#

I don't care if your old man is upstairs, I say, lifting her tight skirt. I want to see them.

She presses into my zipper, pushes up against the root. It's going to cost you, she says.

Halfway up the back of her thighs, I feel satin, drift upward to a bit bare bun I smack. She laughs. What did you say your name was?

#

I can't remember how the shorts got in my room. I flung them off my face when I heard pounding on the door, someone yelling, you're going to miss your train. I intended to pack them but the train to Atlanta was leaving in 12 minutes. I remembered them in Savannah when I wiped my nose and got a whiff of Mississippi crawdad. And in Charleston, at a bar Edgar Allan Poe boozed at, I reopened the file on the biking shorts from Orleans.

That night I got a gum infection.

#

Wife comes home. Well, *what did the bank say?*
In legalese, fuck you.
She smiles, her tired pretty telling me to pour the wine. I do.
Anyone call?
Yeah, coroner from New Orleans.
She takes a big drink. I show her the number. *You call back?*
No.
Why not? She taps in the number, eyes me like I've been hiding something. *You don't have something to tell me, do you?*
Semen and panties, I mutter.
She discards my droll, hangs up. Number's been disconnected.
She pours another. *What's for dinner?*
Semen and panties.
You're such a freak.

#

Next day I start the novel wearing her black thong. Hallelujah.

~Michael Frias-May

CICATRIX

awkward July night
the moon was a crooked smile

in a dead El Camino
we sat
smoking hash

she told me
that she once dressed like a clown
and went down on her ex-boyfriend's
grandpa as a joke

I told her that my uncle Jim
once touched me
in the basement
with an antique catcher's mitt

we fucked like lunatics
howled like wolves
in her eyes
she had fireflies

the next day
I evaporated

she was far too pretty
to shackle to an anvil
like me

~Niall Rasputin

ANNIVERSARY

A year passed
yet you never uttered
a single word,
an oxymoron on acid

Your lips sputter
in ether beds
when the moon
retreats in
mourning
in rose beds,
storm drains

You aren't hither
but you linger –
I hear you
in painted photos
gleaming smile
a bit too pinched

Still you imply:
"Hurry honey –
I can't hold this pose
forever"

But the picture frame tells
the opposite
story
and I feel your touch
under silk sheets
where you hover

the past still visceral

And I can taste
your supple kiss
that emerges
from dampened earth

~ Michael Wayne Holland

FIFTY SHADES OF BULLSHIT

Fifty shades of bullshit got your panties in a bunch
fiction in the place of the real friction of wet thighs
and gravel sighs
and a man's rough hands where you settle for the
touch of your own

Waste of time between life's stages
replaced by dog-eared pages where fantasy isn't real
wax fruit in place of a meal
hot wax on skin like in some video with music and a
grainy feel
story never meant to last like you and I once did

I have read your kind before
a spider web in place of a door
and spilt perfume to cover the decay of what once passed
for your tender soul cracked and old and dry and dying
and lied to by so many, then so few
now just by you

Last look back at a life unfinished
at bodies and minds left diminished
by time, by the past, by struggle against what once
convinced us that we were our last and only
never get lonely partners for life till I saw light

Fifty shades of bullshit got your panties in a bunch
trying to remember what didn't need reading pages
were never meant for feeling what once was between us
heat in the place of a cold feel, of pulp in the space where
you melt cold steel of my rough hands as they touched
what was my own

~Bill Friday

HAND PRINTS IN THE DUST

I'm behind you and we're
rocking together
as head lowered
you concentrate on
this
the
deepest of love.

Your hair falls in front of your pink
flushed
face
as my fullness quickens
producing
judders that resonate through your
soft dewy
sultriness.

You rest your hands on the
sill
the curtains open
to some street
stretching out to
nowhere -
as inside your urgency
rages.

I grip
your hips
while on the bed your
discarded
underwear
lies like promises -

promises
of other days
other
nights.

This vision of our
intimacy
sears
into my conscience
creating
memories that will
remain for ever
as you
whisper my name
over and
over.

Your head
falls
as my passion
floods with your orgasm -
a river of us.

Today
I stand
alone now in this empty room
curtains
flutter
as a lonely wind blows
by.

Is it your
perfume
or the sad wind
blowing?

are they your
foot prints indented
in the carpet?
are they your finger prints
in the dust?
Faint
now in my lonely
recollection
I try to capture the hint of
Dior's Poison
in the air and
place my feet just behind
yours.

I
softly retrace your tiny
hand prints in the dust
as outside lonely church bells
ring.

~Roger Cornish

LIFTED, BY A STRANGER'S HAND

Some cheap thrills
Are like no other
Perfected by my reckless lover
With each response
She does confess
The tell-tale signs
Of her dress
Lifted by a stranger's hand
He slipped his fingers
Through her sand
Now deserts build upon our bed
From your oasis
I was led
To drink from the holy water
That flows with guilt
From the altar
Where vows were made
And secrets kept
Upon the sheets
Where we once slept
Lifted by a stranger's hand
The rhythmic motion
Of his command
Commands me to
To watch and learn
The wage of lust
I've had to earn
Is like his kiss
Upon your breast
The endless kiss
That knows no rest

Is given here
To no surprise
What I have learned
Will not make me wise

~Spencer Slater

CONDENSED MILK

She holds a gaggle of reproof
bunched in her rolled up panties,
on my couch by the moonlight sonata
and the hatched chirping nest eggs,
instructing me on everything I didn't know
from the wrong smelling candlelight
to the metric ton dinner.
So tired of her snaggletooth antics,
I must remain aloof, so aloof,
trace a heart in the sand of her Zen garden
to get her legs pointing at the roof.

She bought me chicken fingers
at Studebakers, yeah, that's how we met.
She dressed up like a kitten, a teardrop
expanding excitement on her tongue.
I was Zorro, equally in ecstasy,
grinding bodies on the dance floor,
covered in iridescent sweat.
I spoke to her in condensed milk
language and whippoorwill voice.
Kissing in her trusty Cadillac,
policeman tapping on the glass,
I thought of Son of Sam
pointing a gun with a dog bark
which almost gave me a heart attack.

She bought me jalapeño poppers
at Horsefeathers, this repeating way we met,
grinding bodies in the alley stinking of sweat.
Fucking in her rusty Pontiac,
a thunderclap rattling the glass

138

almost gave me a heart attack.
She whimpers a silent reproof
and doesn't bother pulling up her panties.
I'm so tired of her apathetic antics
that I must remain more aloof
than any wise graffiti glowing on the roof.

~Angel Uriel Perales

FLYING

Tired is the jumping off point,
the ledge on which she stands
remembering the bounce
of high board at the swimming hole
where she entertained him nightly
when he was still a boy
and she a femme fatale,
intent on being different
noticed, worshipped, adored,
tease-stripping, tossing her garments
onto the limbs of trees.

There is no bounce where she now stands
only rough edge tempting,
teasing her weary toes
turned inward, pre- takeoff.
She's letting go at last,
abandoning the dream
their destinations are the same,
flinging her clothes before
the thousand eyes of night.
They fall softly over fir trees
in this hymnless season of dying.

~Barbara Moore

WE MADE LOVE IN THE ETHER BEFORE FLESH

we made love in the ether before flesh
or form we made love to a bombshell
on a sound wave across the room we made love
to a cricket serenade we made love on the beach in the ocean
on vacation in meditation on medication we made love
in the shower in the tub in a tea cup
thimble puddle pint glass pool of blind faith
we made love on the wall in the stairwell
in your hair on the high rise boot
of your finest italian leather we made love
with a camera vibrator corn dog can
of extra heavy whipping cream we made love
before we knew our names we made love with our hats
holsters and spurs on we made love with our designer
genes on we made love with the lights tv stereo
future plans past promises & present masks on
over & over & over & under
& in between we made love in a clinging
whiplash spasm all hazy afternoon we made love
at 40,000 feet above the hand to mouth rat race
madness reflex we made love before we crossed
the threshold we made love in the cradle
of death valley in the basement fury of your holy land
mind field cloudburst current on a lightning strike
hurricane bed we made love in a bed of poison ivy
we made love in the fifteen minute motel we
made love in an irish castle on a blackhole mattress
with a million ghosted impressions we made love
at the crossroads of childbirth & divorce
&then we added a chapter to the kama sutra
under the table at that indian restaurant we made love

in a cheap bottle of sweet hangover wine
& we made love for no reason
but love on the moonbeam
of god's flashlight

~Stephen Roxborough

MERCIES TENDERED

man & woman meet in relief,
stripping themselves of the ghosts they wear

pain no longer lingers, fear no longer resides
behind burning eyes passion & promise are found
where healing begins from mobius within mobius

ouroborus recoiled shapes conjoined hearts
exquisite welcome transcends silent sufferance
in the desideratum of the delta of venus between

earthly bodies held high from the depths
of clandestine grieving where man & woman
collide in unexpected recognition,

igniting under the searing eyes of stained-glass gods

~Alicia Winski

AN OTHER DREAMS OF SPRING

> *Mixed days, the mindless years, perceived*
> *With half-parted lips*
> *The way the breath of spring creeps up on you and floors you.*
> *I had thought of all this years before*
> *But now it was making no sense. And the song had finished …*
> *~ John Ashbery, "The Double Dream of Spring"*

helixed

days, blind mindless years,

unperceived with dream, …

                  indwelling

                        ice locked

half-parted lips in night transfiguration

enswayment light breath end light   instantiation

countenance convection love,

                psychic reverberation

]in[im]perfection spring creeps radiant   buoyant

comprehension births

                psychic reverberation

of night, mindstorm reborn,

                psychic reverberation

archetype sh]oar[es you

moored wintered

his shadow her benign light transfiguration

incountenance through love,

                psychic reverberation

perfection with all, …

                psychic reverberation

years before

              her body a flame with the scent of love

now prana world, *nee* trauma world
apocalyptic hiding behind the wor⌐l⌐ds

                  making sense-less elliptic return

                     an other dreams of spring
mindstorm reborn,

        her body a fire in a waterfall of flowers

           psychic reverberation
archetype light song refinished:

           psychic reverberation
errant light story :: in past

          tense   tenses
helix entwines mirrors you
finds men
with dream, …

      i⌐u⌐ndwelling

      psychic starlight mindstorm reborn,

           psychic reverberation
archetype third eyes
among u⌐i⌐ncertainty islands
primal in time and i⌐u⌐nlove
light transfiguration redesign incompletes
apocalyptic hiding behind the wor⌐l⌐ds

            making sense-less ecliptic foreshadow
a life lived to describe an elliptic

                an other dreams of spring

      mindstorm reborn,

        mindstorm reborn,

          mindstorm reborn,

           where words

are growing things   psychic reverberation
        disetiolating dreams in moonlight

  archetype one keeps walking down
pushing up through light's concrete
      curling out away from their roots
awaiting their blooms
      genetic breath light shore
footsteps searching prana world
      where words   are growing things
]yet they shan't have prana world[
        and music is their rain
    poems   *b r e a t h e*
between the wafting notes
        take me again and again
        play the black keys of my heart
        with the fingers of your tongue
a formal prana world
     ]dis[possessed
      children's voices their starlight
]dis[possessed light spray to tune consciousness
      whistling
      rampaging destiny way
        mindstorm reborn,
     psychic reverberation
    becoming moonlight's etiolation
   muscles peeling ecstasy
unraveling the psychic core
with archetype, …

transmogrification
we keep stepping ...
down ...

light transfiguration rowboat rocked helix entwines mirrors
I stepped eye scanning desolation prana worlds; terrained trauma
worlds descendant antecedent light transfiguration]sh[oars pushed
away reforming light small waves spanning matrix unleashed forbidden
fears forbidden desires reverbrant face fade blood orchid blooming]un[
her nipples on fire swim the scent of love
with water, ...
light, ...
with light, ...
waves, ...
with waves, ...
"end of the journey" quantumness, ...
with quantumness, ...
beginning of journey
possessions]dis[position
mindstorm reborn,
probing, flicking, lapping the poem of sweetheatsweat&desire
her vulva shrieking in the hurricane of tongues
words are living things
psychic reverberation
unfolding from their phonemes
apocalyptic hiding behind the wor]l[ds
making sense-less rife with aural blossom
life lived to describe an elliptic   an other dreams of spring
mindstorm reincarnate,

                                        dying matrices of the wor[l]ds reborn
carbon chased life form wriggles ash(oar)e
archetype projects outward, blinded re: turns
genetic breath examining
                              an other dreams
of spring,
matrix unleashed forbidden
light stream. language swirls
with prana world, …
                          dream transfiguration
coursing matrix unleashed forbidden light scree
rampage destiny remade light voice stand, shout, spray
with dream, …
                    indwelling
                    dream song, dream light
                                  peculiar coherency.
radiant comprehension
            regenerate
            elongation within, …
                                ecliptic
                    psychic reverberation
night (f)light aurora (a)light transfiguration
road to psychic anarchy   bled
                    her feet kissed by an erection of heartache
                    her mouth surrounds the penile head
incertainty light sidestorm   fled
genetic breath dream song, dream light
]col[l]ective[ap][se]point somewhere beyond theself
caught, lost matrix unleashed

                    elongation within, …
forbidden billions in light   transfiguration
sustained countenance through love,
                    psychic reverberation
perfection sea-analogies
being light furthest step one might find

    the point is not to demarcate a line
        rather

                                transfiguration
mind
storm reborn her skin steaming in the lucidity of passion
                her (m)embers gripped glowing in the seething tongs
                her clitoris smoldering under the hammer of the tongue
                    psychic reverberation
archetype amid ago light
chur(n)rings in light now transfiguration
incountenance through love,   her pussy aching
                    psychic reverberation
reflected dreamship intercurrent
radiant comprehension seducing
                    psychic reverberation
night light land light grass lies over passive
                                words
                        are living things
                                opening up
                                from ethereal nothingness
inseminating prana worlds "send light transfiguration countenance
            through

love   this   this   this

perfection echoes light journey" mentality spanning desolation creased
forehead

echoes where love is

an impatiens insurrection

a rebellion of roses

a jasmine revolution

apocalyptic hiding behind the wor]l[ds

making sense-less

her life loved to describe an ecliptic   an other dreams of spring

mindstorm reborn, retraced

from gene,   making sense-less

this   this   this   holy reincarnate possibility

awashed psychic starlight in vitro finning reenvisioned

smelling of ethereal tides, fragranseas in[de]scented oceans

archetype starlight radiant comprehension

riot of the jasmine revolution

marching love&peace

through the no-man's-womb

of war-born]e[destiny

religion&death-torn *kyrie*

an other dreams of spring

psychic reverberation

une Dèesse verte perceiving herself into being

roan goddess polyvulvular siren singing lush litany of lilacs

her cunt]be[coming in a lucidity of flowers

rampaging beauty instantiated in-dwelling

                her desire hot fountain erupting & probing
night rampage seed pecking aureole inseminate
                her ripe nipples asong explode drifting swans
sweet creamy breasts mercuring within melting feathers
angelic destiny remirroring inviolate rebudding
incantate substrata blooms pollinate prana
worlds mesmeric ago again

dna entwines carbon
day springs up
awakens
helix
kiss
                        ind[s]welling
this
  in
    vitro
          labian
                water

                fall

                bliss

                        a
                         f
                         i
                        re

~Michael Annis

Photo Credits

Naked Couple Embracing ©1001nights – iStockphotos.com Quotation Page
Untitled ©Alexis Rhone Fancher Page 8
Nude Body Scape © Katrina Brown – Fotolia.com   Page 11
Gymnastic Nude © Ben Heyes – Fotolia.com Page 32
Concept of Yin and Yang © Wisky – Fotolia.com Page 45
Mary Fae Smith © Alexis Rhone Fancher Page 73
Untitled © ruslimonchyk – Fotolia.com Page 75
Untitled © Alexis Rhone Fancher Page 100
Couple Kissing & Embracing © coloroftime – iStockphotos.com Page 143

Publishing Credits In Order of Appearance

tosaíonn an aisling

www.ingramcontent.com/pod-product-compliance
Lightning Source LLC
Chambersburg PA
CBHW071343090426
42738CB00012B/2996